MW00809762

SHOE ARE YOU?

DESIGN
Peter Ratcliffe
www.peterratcliffe.com

10 9 8 7 6 5 4 3 2 1

MISS MEGHAN MEDIA
8033 SUNSET BOULEVARD, SUITE 993
LOS ANGELES, CA 90046

www.missmeghan.com

DEDICATION

*To all the women around
the world who have shared
their shoe stories with me*

Chapter three

ON-THE-GO

Chapter four

TOWERING HEIGHTS

INTRODUCTION

I am passionate about shoes. Since I was five and discovered my first pair of baby blue wedge espadrille sandals with embroidery on the toebox, I have had many a shoe moment throughout my lifetime. As I grew older, Shoe Money was a literal term for me - I worked on Wall Street, and spent my money on shoes. I had a pair of red sparkly red slingbacks that I used as a table centerpiece for six months before I could bear to put them on the city streets. I scoured vintage shops in the East Village for the perfect Stiletto silhouette from the 60s - and when the heel snapped off, I lovingly encased it in plastic and put it on display. My West Village apartment became a shoe merchandising heaven as I constantly thought up new ways to display six-inch navy patent platform pumps by hanging them off bookshelves, or stringing my favorite stilettos on the rungs of an eight-foot ladder in my foyer.

I have been all over the world in the name of shoes. I have visited with Italian designers in their studios, have been flown to London to see the first ever musical devoted to shoes, and have even had my shoe musings translated into Croatian! I have had the wonderful opportunity to discover and report on some of the most exciting, up-and-coming shoe designers worldwide. I have studied footwear trends and their impact on culture and society, and had the privilege of talking with thousands and thousands of women from Paris to Zagreb, London to Milan, New York to Sydney about their shoe desires, shoe moods and shoe stories. My passion for shoes and what they say about you never wanes.

Shoes, unlike anything else we put on our body, have an actual physiological impact on us: shoes affect the way we walk, carry ourselves and stand. Shoes are central to our moods as women, to our identity, and how we feel in the moment.

So, Shoe are You?
In your hands you hold an entertaining look into what your shoes reveal about you. First, we'll identify your Shoe Sun sign -- your essential shoe personality. Then we go on to your Shoe Rising sign, explore a few shoe opposites and maybe even identify a few areas of your life you need to explore as indicated by your shoe choices. Or if you want, delve straight into reading about whatever shoe sign interests you.

I am so excited about sharing my shoe passion with you, and hope you enjoy this shoe adventure.

Meghan Cleary

WHAT EXACTLY IS A STILETTO?

The word "stiletto" originates from the lovely Latin word stylus, meaning "slender dagger." Doesn't that just send naughty shivers up your spine? Believed to have been created for Catherine de Medici in the 1530s by an unnamed Florentine artisian, stilettos had their rebirth in 1955 when Roger Vivier designed a pointy, high heel fortified with a thin metal heel tube for Dior. This meant that we could enjoy the swaying seductive walk stilettos offered, with minimum breakage; this was the precursor of the luscious stiletto we enjoy today, which has been made even more durable with the advent of space-age plastic!

It is said that the shape of a woman's foot in a stiletto mimics the shape of the leg and foot during extreme sexual arousal, which is a delicious little tidbit to think about. At the very least, a stiletto always gets you to strike a pose, however unconsciously, and turns you into the natural seductress you are.

Chapter one

SHOE ARE YOU?

Like star signs, shoe girls fall into basic categories: In this case, Down-to-Earth, On-the-Go, and Towering Heights. Chapters 2, 3, and 4 further define these types, as well as offer the related shoe signs and personality descriptors. Feel free to dive into any of the shoe chapters ahead, or, if you want to dig in a little deeper, answer all the questions in Chapter 1 to really get sole-searching.

First, Shoe are You?

1. What is your absolute favorite pair of shoes?

2. Give me three adjectives that come to mind when you think of these shoes. *(example: comfortable, expensive, drop-dead gorgeous)*.

3. Now give me three adjectives that describe how you feel when you wear these shoes. *(example: I feel joyous, confident, sexy)*.

4. What are three compliments you've received from friends and admiring observers about these shoes?
(example: You sexy thing! Where did you find those? Your legs go on forever!).

5. Flip through the next three chapters in the book to find the shoe that most closely matches your favorite shoe. Then, write that shoe type here.

Waxing & Waning

Women are creatures of many moods
and feelings. Your Shoe Sun sign may not
be a single constant. Ask yourself Shoe are You?
but ask it at a specific time of day, specific day
of the week, or in a certain season. It is very likely your
Friday night shoe is different than your Monday morning
shoes. Your Saturday afternoon in the yard shoes,
are very different than your Tuesday going
to a business meeting shoes. Your mid-winter
shoe choice, different than your early fall.

SHOE DO YOU WANT TO BE?

Women are complex creatures. Your Shoe Sun sign, while certainly the main character, is not the whole story. So tell me,

Shoe do you want to be?

1. What is the last pair of shoes you wanted to buy but didn't? Perhaps you went so far as to bring them home but later returned them in a fit of self-doubt?

2. Flip through the book to find the type of shoe that most closely matches the shoe you nearly bought. Then write that shoe type here. *(Don't be surprised if it's a stiletto. I have found many women naturally incline toward their inner Stiletto.)*

3. Give me three positive adjectives to describe these shoes you didn't buy. *(example: comfy, hot, sleek).*

4. Now, three negative adjectives that describe these shoes *(example: expensive, trendy, uncomfortable).*

*The shoe you've just identified
is your Shoe Rising sign,
the state of shoe you aspire to.
It is important to note that
you may have several shoe rising
signs, so repeat the questionnaire
as the mood strikes.
The positive adjectives you list
identify aspects of your life
that might need some attention.
The negative adjectives identify
specific resistances you may have.
Identifying your Shoe Rising
sign is key to moving beyond
where you are now
and charting a path toward
where you want to go.*

MOVING BEYOND YOUR FEARS

Go to Question 4 on page 8;
"Shoe do you want to be?"
Now, see if any of those adjectives
you wrote down match the
adjectives I have listed on the
next page. Underneath each adjective,
you'll find my advice.

OUTRAGEOUS, SCANDALOUS, SHOCKING

You may be suppressing an innate desire to wear colorful,
wild shoes to the office. But sometimes you have to let go
and take a walk on the wild side.

FRIVOLOUS, CHILDISH, SILLY

You may need a bit more fun in your life.
Get in touch with your inner whimsy. Leave what you are doing
right now and run to the store where you saw those shoes.
Buy them, take them home, and then put on
an entire outfit worthy of these shoes!

EXPENSIVE, EXTRAVAGANT

Let's talk about value and cost-per-wear. Did you know every time
you wear that pair of shoes, you cut the cost in half, and then in
half again? Don't be risky with your funds, but do recognize value.
The cheap always pay twice!

STRANGE, BIZARRE

How about unique? You picked them up for a reason.
Unusual design, texture, or shape may be just what I would
order for you. It's good to push the envelope on what you think
is conventional. Keeps you on your toes, so to speak.

TOO HIGH

Believe me, I understand too high. Shoe manufacturers have increased the average height of a high heel two inches over the last decade - oftentimes leading us to wonder, is it me or is it this shoe? However, if you NEVER wear high heels, and are drawn to a high heel, it can be valuable to just stand in one, even for a little while. Feel how it feels to tower, the difference in how your carry yourself. Pay attention to that - this is key for paying attention to the power inside yourself you might want to tap into.

TOO LOW

Are you are a high-heel junkie? Some time closer to the earth may be what you secretly crave. And don't worry, you're not selling yourself short. Feeling the earth move under your feet could be just the vibe you're looking for.

NOT DESIGNER

Uh-oh. Looks like a serious case of designer-itis. You've got to mix the high and low cultures to have fun, my friend.

BRIGHT, COLORFUL

Baby, you need some diversity in your life. You may not find an everyday use for that pair of kelly-green python pumps or those purple suede stilettos, but that doesn't mean they don't belong in your wardobe.

OPPOSITES ATTRACT

Yes, there is such a thing as an Opposite Shoe sign. Find your Shoe Sun sign in the following chart. The shoe beside it is your Opposite Shoe sign. Opposites are a great tool for sole discovery, as they identify a path that deserves a little exploration and inner reflection. Do you consciously resist your Opposite? Do you have any friends who are Opposite? Read your Opposite's profile in Chapters 2, 3, or 4 and think seriously about what this says about you. I recommend you go so far as to seek out a pair of Opposites and wear them for at least a day. Before you judge, walk a mile in those shoes.

SHOE SUN SIGN	OPPOSITE SHOE SIGN
Barefoot	Platform Shoe
Flip-Flop	Ankle Boot with High-Heel
Reef Sandal	Mule with High-Heel
Classic Leather Thong Sandal	Pointy Toe Skimmer
Ballet Flat	Cowboy Boot
Australian Sheep Boot	Classic Conservative Pump
T-Strap	Clog
Retro Basketball	Loafer
Minimalist	Oxford Wingtip
Running Shoe	Open Toe
High-Heel Sandal	Hiking Boot
Stiletto	Orthopedic Sandal
Sneaker	Knee-High Boot with Heel
Knee-High Boot with Low Heel	Bedroom Slipper
Mary Jane	Workingman's Boot

INVOKING YOUR INNER STILETTO

When I talk about your Inner Stiletto, what I really mean is your core feminine brilliance. For each of you lovely ladies, I wanted to give you a little tip on how to bring out your gorgeousness just a little more for your specific shoe sign. Invoking your Inner Stiletto is a way to really turn things up a notch, no matter what shoe sign you are.

Chapter two

DOWN-TO-EARTH

The women who inhabit the Down-to-Earth category like to feel grounded and in step with reality at all times. The feel of the earth or pavement beneath your feet gives you a feeling of stability that helps you move through life with a very consistent and steady pace, approaching all situations with holistic understanding. For you in this category, dressing up is more about letting your inner beauty shine than about giving an everyday show.

BAREFOOT

You fancy yourself a naturalist, a hippie, or someone who just doesn't belong in shoes. Whatever your reason, you, the Barefoot girl, have eschewed shoes. You are eminently charming and lovable, carefree and breezy, and you usually add a breath of fresh air to any room you enter (sometimes along with a slight breeze of lavender-verbena aromatherapy).

You may have discovered your love of barefootedness in early childhood, when shoes restricted your natural independent spirit: you pleaded to go barefoot just another hour in the summer or into the fall, when most other children were slipping back into school shoes. Because your independence started early and is deeply ingrained in your sense of self, it is important that you are around those who value your free-spirited sensibility, for you can open their eyes to a whole new world.

Your friendships are formed with those who appreciate your grounded independence and correspond with more earth-centered issues like environmentalism and vegetarianism. However, you are very tolerant of all different walks of life. Since you yourself are considered a bit odd, you often befriend those who also need a bit of cheering from the outside world. A loyal friend, though sometimes hard to pin down, you will always be there, with many a natural remedy on hand, in any kind of crisis.

Traveling far and wide, you live in many different places, in search of new things to catch your eye and light up your idealism. Constant change is a fixed phenomenon in your lifestyle.

⭐ *completing the look*

Try breezy flowing skirts that do not hinder movement. Your hair, long and loose, looks nice tied up in a natural hemp ponytail holder, with tendrils slipping out. For makeup, try organic olive-oil soap and fresh aloe, and cherry-flavored lip gloss. Earrings are long and flowy and usually handmade (try the ones you picked up in that Southwestern town you lived in for a while) by a local artisan. Try wearing a few rings made out of natural fibers and sometimes an ankle bracelet or two, which tinkle quietly as you enter the room.

📱 *work it, girl*

Go for what your heart leads you to, what is right instinctively both for you and for a larger cause. You'll work tirelessly, but you must be mentally engaged and a true believer in whatever task you take on. An occupation that gives you flexibility, freedom, and an unstructured environment is always preferred. Volunteering at the local food co-op or Habitat for Humanity, marching in a rally for peace, and working on voter registration are good projects. Varied tasks are key, as boredom is a great danger for your spirit. Interacting with people and using your hands are also important.

🐾 *finding a sole mate*

While loving just as freely as you meander, you are not indiscriminate. Your loves are as heartfelt, sweet, and pure as that third-grade crush. You fall hard and are often disappointed, for you have extremely high ideals when it comes to love. Learning to manage your expectations in order to be happy and fulfilled in love is a key challenge. Your mate must have ideals as high as yours when it comes to believing in the goodness of the world and being engaged in life at a visceral level. A mate with a bit of practicality might benefit you, a little yin for your yang.

INVOKING YOUR INNER STILETTO

Try a touch of organic sandalwood essential oil behind your ears. Known to induce lust in even the most stoic of individuals, it's a great way for you to turn it up a notch.

famous

BAREFOOT GIRLS

MICHELLE PHILLIPS *The Mamas and the Papas,*
GOLDIE HAWN *in Butterflies Are Free,*
JOSS STONE

BEDROOM SLIPPER

You are a bit dreamy, half awake, half asleep. Your moniker is cozy. Often seen curled up on the couch in front of a daytime movie or just sipping your first cup of morning tea, you are surrounded by icons of comfort: flannel sheets, soft blankets, chocolate ice cream, lots of body lotion in lavender or green apple. Your movements are slow and languorous, with an innate sensuality you are almost unaware of, but inhabit with the inner assurance of an eighteenth-century courtesan.

★ completing the look

Flannel or very soft well-worn cotton jersey-knit PJs are a must in pink, white, soft yellow, or mint green. Your hair is unwashed and often sticking up in some places, and makeup is clear lip balm and a rich face moisturizer. No jewelry and a slight natural rose flush colors the cheeks.

📱 work it, girl

You are not working — you are relaxing.

💘 finding a sole mate

Your mates are entranced by your dedication to comfort. You are the epitome of all earthly senses in their fully relaxed state. In order for your mates to understand you, they've got to get into the Zen vibe, too. You live in another world, where things take time, and as soon as your mates understand this, they will be as relaxed and happy as you are.

INVOKING YOUR INNER STILETTO

*Slip into a transparent vintage
nightie instead of your PJs -
just as soft and sensual.
Paired with your bedroom slippers,
it's the best of comfy and sexy.*

FLIP FLOP

More often than not, you are on a boat or a dock. Very likely, you grew up on the water in a coastal town and know a sailboat like the back of your hand. Energetic and permanently tanned, you are a strong hand to have aboard any vessel. You can read a wave like a born surfer, and you like to race. Steady as a rudder, you are loyal and true to your good friends and in fact prefer their company après-sail to large social occasions. Having been in many a sea or Great Lake adventure, you sparkle with the energy of being truly alive, an intoxicating quality.

★ completing the look

Because you're so at home on the water, shorts and a tank top over a swimsuit become your natural elements of choice. Your hair, usually bleached a bit by the sun, can be thrown up in a messy ponytail or bun to keep it from interfering when you pull the jib. Since you've got an easy, natural beauty, the only makeup you need is sunscreen and a lip protectant.

📱 work it, girl

You've got to be engaged with water to be happy, so marine biologist, whale-watch tour guide, dockhand, and competitive sailor are all good matches to keep your spirits up and your energy fluid.

💘 finding a sole mate

Your mate has got to love the water, obviously. In addition, you need to be with someone you admire, who secretly is your hero, whether because of coming in first in the America's Cup or knowing how to tie a knot with ease.

INVOKING YOUR INNER STILETTO

*Suncreen of course is a must
for whatever mood you are in.
So add a little sheen in that screen.
A tiny bit of sparkle on
your skin gives you extra gleam.*

AUSTRALIAN SHEEP BOOT

You are one notch above bedroom slipper girl in that you are about that relaxed, but you take it outside the house. College campus, city street, beach or on-set between takes, you've got the mellow rolling walk that is almost sloppy, even if you are scurrying to class because you are late. These boots automatically put the brakes on moving at any kind of top speed. You are willing to sacrifice any kind of conventional style for the belief that your boot's cozy interior sheepskin more than makes up for any fashion statement you could be making. In some ways, you turn your sloppy boot into the anti-fashion statement, speaking volumes about your beliefs of function over form.

★ completing the look

It's casual, comfy and cozy all the way for you, unless you are aprés-ski or aprés-surf in which case you are in your ski gear or bikini. One step above pajamas works for you. Leggings, a worn-in denim mini with or without cozy tights, supersoft skinny jeans, jersey t-shirts that drape, and cashmere sweater pullovers or cardigans, tanks so old they might be slightly transparent, a knit unstructured dress-pieces that are unstructured, soft and cozy, cozy, cozy. For makeup, botanical lip gloss, a spot of creme blush and a lick of mascara just about does it and hair is down or in a messy bun on top of head.

📱 work it, girl

Going from English to Math class on campus - student life agrees with you. You might be an actress between takes on-set of your latest movie or TV show, or a writer on deadline, a PhD. student working to finish up her thesis. You might be a visual artist installing your latest work at a gallery, you could be in a science lab in Anarctica, or a champion skier.

🏃 finding a sole mate

You need a partner who is cool with completely casual, and by that I mean they are totally comfortable with you whatever you turn up in. Definitely not someone who is high maintenance or requires too much fussing over - very down-to-earth.

INVOKING YOUR INNER STILETTO

[*If it's a cardigan, make it the most body-hugging-fits-you-like-a-glove cashmere. Now, revel in every caress.*]

REEF SANDAL

You find yourself in reef sandals more than any other shoe and are therefore both sturdy and adventurous. You have many a trip to the Amazon and endangered tropical rain forests under your belt, and always ready for the next one, you radiate the energy of the perpetual traveler. You engineer modern public-health systems in developing countries as easily as you board the seaplane to your next destination. Unconcerned with material trappings, you believe that your next meal, house, or clothing will manifest itself without too much worry.

★ completing the look

Step out in easy, flexible pieces that wash well in any kind of water. All-natural cotton and moisture-wicking fabrics are important, in colors that are spirited: turquoise, purples, printed white tees, and tank tops. A swimsuit not only is for swimming but also is an integral extra layer, so multiple mix-and-match suits with durable construction are important. To easily camouflage the effect of limited showers, hair should be kept long. Makeup in the form of sunscreen and lip gloss complete the look.

📱 work it, girl

Ecotour leader. Your flair for adventure and your keen mind lead you to professions in which both intimate knowledge of geography and skill in traveling over rugged terrain are important. White-water rafting expeditions and rain-forest adventures are also great opportunities for you to apply your skills.

🐾 finding a sole mate

You need to be with a fellow adventurer, one who can bivouac with you through the mountainous terrain of life: a mate who is taken with natural beauty, has the unflagging spirit of a pioneer, and is physically hardy. A sense of humor is key so that you can laugh together at the latest Amazonian downpour from inside your tent.

INVOKING YOUR INNER STILETTO

You're in the tropical rain forest,
which is quite like a sauna.
For your next adventure,
try a polka-dot bikini,
keep your sandals, slather
on the bug repellent and toss
the rest into the jungle.

ORTHOPEDIC SANDAL

Often startlingly beautiful, your glowing complexion may be the first thing that strikes a person upon meeting you. Because you are probably a vegan, the fruits and veggies you consume every day give you a natural, radiant glow. To the unenlightened, you may come across as complacent, but you shouldn't be underestimated. It's not that you are oblivious to the world around you, it's just that you see everything a little differently. Where one might see barren trees, you see stark beauty. Where one might see a thunderstorm, you see proof of nature's grace. Get the picture? Because of your ethereal nature, you are calming to be around. Though it may be an adjustment for those in your company to slow down enough to hang with you, they will find it well worth their while as you transmit to them a bit of your everyday joy - quite a nice feeling.

★ completing the look

Try flowered, flowing skirts, easy drawstring pants in a solid cotton, a soft tank top or oversize man's button-down shirt, knotted at the waist or thrown over your ensemble. Denim overalls and a wife beater are an easy way to inhabit your oeuvre as well. Hair is long or a chin-length bob, often pulled back in a headband or ponytail. Flavored lip gloss in a variety of all-natural fruity scents is all the makeup you need.

📱 work it, girl

You are quite relaxed when it comes to working, always believing that things will work themselves out organically. Occupations in which you can engage with the natural world are recommended, be it a health-food co-op, a gardening gig, exterior housepainting, forestry or environmental work, or even involvement with Greenpeace. Since you may be a bit of the hidden artist, working on large outdoor sculpture, or painting nature landscape, would be beneficial. Rat-race 9-to-5 jobs are not recommended — they will kill your spirit in moments.

🐾 finding a sole mate

Your mate has to be as dedicated to unstructured living as you are: someone with solid values, who is well-read, extremely understanding, and a bit quiet, though a mate who can really make your inner sweet giggle emerge is valuable, too. For that reason, playfulness is key in your equation of love.

INVOKING YOUR INNER STILETTO

*Let's lay the sandals aside
for a moment and go
barefoot, non? A little
oil of sandalwood, perhaps?
(See Barefoot, page 17.)*

CLASSIC LEATHER THONG SANDAL

You take a resort attitude to life. Your pace is unhurried island time, a slower, more meditative approach. If it doesn't get done today, it can always get done tomorrow, or next week, for that matter. While others may get temporarily frustrated at your seeming lack of regard for their pace of life, they should actually be thankful, for you are the embodiment of the natural rhythm we should all strive for.

★ completing the look

Complete your look with a maxi skirt of cotton or linen and a tank top. Cotton shorts or clam diggers with a formfitting tee in solid colors is a nice ensemble for you as well. Accessorize with a wide-brimmed straw hat and a bright tote for daily shopping. Your hair, short or long, is cut in layers and flowing or up in a casual bun. Makeup is a sheer pink lip gloss and a subtle glow in the cheek.

📱 work it, girl

You've got to be in a flexible profession that allows you to enjoy open and airy spaces. A massage therapist or Pilates teacher at a luxury spa in an exotic locale, a high-fashion model on location, a photographer for a travel magazine, or even the owner of the local surf shop: all fit you well.

🌸 finding a sole mate

Look for a mate who embodies the attitude of a surfer (if not one already!). Someone who appreciates a slower pace, interested in the innate beauty and organic rhythm of life. Your mate should be able to laugh at absurdity just as easily as swinging into downward dog next to you on the yoga mat. Physically sturdy and fit, you and your mate should have a healthy dose of respect for each other.

INVOKING YOUR INNER STILETTO

Step out of your natural rhythm and just for an hour, speed things up to see how the rest of the world operates. When you come back to your natural tempo, you will be all the more appreciative of the way you approach life. Now breathe in and ahhhhh, exhale.

MINIMALIST

Active, active, active. You are scaling rock walls, leading a pilates class, hiking a canyon or rassling your kids around town. You like to feel the earth beneath your feet but are also practical enough to know that you've got to have a little protection on your foot, i.e. you are interested in the biomechanic benefits of walking and running this way. To be happy, you have to be moving and using every bone in your body to its maximum capacity.

★ completing the look

You like activewear, fabrics and materials that are easy, somewhat bold in color and well-cut for ease of movement. Hair is either short or swept up in a messy bun or ponytail, rarely down all the way. A smudge of lip balm with SPF, some super sport deodorant and sometimes a little creme blush is all you do in the way of a beauty regime, keeping it simple and on the go. Mix up your everyday wardrobe with some sleek yoga pants or leggings, some vibrant hats and layer tanks.

📱 work it, girl

You have got to be doing something that keeps you engaged - yes you can work in an office but you must be out early to be able to hike or mountain bike after work. Better jobs for you are more flexible ones that either have you outside part of the time and a looser schedule - adventure guide, personal fitness trainer training clients outdoors, rock climbing specialist or working at an outdoor adventure store - either on the store floor or in corporate, running the show. You are at home both in showing people how to do things and giving them instruction, to running things in the executive suite.

🏇 finding a sole mate

Find someone who is as physically energetic as you are. They have got to have the same level of energy and be just a passionate about keeping it moving. Hopefully they will have an adventurous spirit as well and will be both a support to you when out and about, as well as push you to be the best you can be.

INVOKING YOUR INNER STILETTO

Take things down to a screeching halt
- by that I mean, take five minutes
where you are not doing anything
and let your hair out of your ponytail.
Feel how it feels in every muscle
of your body to be still. 5, 4, 3 ,2 , 1 . . .
Ok, now go!

BALLET FLAT

With a classic streak running though your veins, you either grew up in round-toe ballet flats or recently discovered some in your mother's closet while searching for vintage finds. For all your penchant for funky vintage looks, you are a daddy's girl, brought up with strong middle-class values. You excelled at school, but not in any brainiac kind of way, mostly because you worked hard and were polite to all of your teachers and kind to your classmates. Very often the class president, encouraged to run by your fellow classmates more than by any burning desire to be a political leader, you always had a steady boyfriend, a guy who was just as upstanding as you, and just as nice. You're the one who irons out disagreements between friends, sometimes without their even knowing it, and always with a lot of love. You are the core of any group of girlfriends, and as sweet as you are, you've been known to pull an outrageous prank or two when the conditions were ripe!

★ completing the look

Pair your ballet flats with a tailored designer jean. A solid-color very soft tee and a jacket that is figure-flattering and extremely feminine, often with a floppy silk flower pin on the lapel, completes the look. Makeup is simple and clean, tinted moisturizer so natural you just appear to have flawless skin and that rosy glow. Jewelry is diamond studs. For evening, don a pair of sparkly ballet flats and a sparkly top to match; still in the jeans, you'll give a look of elegance and modernity at the same time.

📱 work it, girl

You like a bit of structure in your life, even if you're at a funky downtown design firm. For that reason, an office environment appeals to you. Try fields in which your ethics will shine and your creativity can be nurtured. A nonprofit working on behalf of the less fortunate, children, or art is a good place to land. Private companies in fashion, graphic, or interior design that give back to the community are also recommended.

💘 finding a sole mate

A mate who can put you at ease is crucial. Someone who is confident, a bit teasing, and funny at the same time is perfect, as you appreciate teasing as a sign of affection. You need to be with mates who are worthy of your time and attention and will make you proud to stand next to them. Above average in looks, your mate needs to adore you profoundly for you to feel happy.

INVOKING YOUR INNER STILETTO

Lacy. Lacy. Lacy.
Camisole, bra, panties,
earrings. Voilà!

MARY JANE

The Mary Jane girl's heart almost always harkens back to the era where girls were girls and boys were boys, and life ticked along with regularity. You like order and neatness in all things, though you are often game for a fun activity (provided it's not too outlandish) and have a great sense of playfulness underneath your prim and proper exterior. You may even pull the occasional complicated practical joke - extremely well orchestrated, of course. But that won't come until you know your victims quite well. You think the colors pale pink, yellow, and mint green are primary colors. Coordination is also a theme with you. In your mind, there is absolutely no reason that one's umbrella, trench coat, and rubber rain boots (I know you wear rubber rain boots on rainy days before you change into your Mary Janes indoors) shouldn't coordinate. Same with your kitchen - freshly lined kitchen shelves stocked with friendly, serviceable cups and saucers in coordinating colors are de rigueur. In your bedroom, English country is the mainstay: coordinated duvet, sheets, curtains, and rug. Fortunately, you have very good taste, so the overall effect of the coordinating is more cheery and comfy than overwhelming. Your belief is that there is no reason not to have a little coordination in one's life, a very calming effect.

★ completing the look

A freshly starched blouse and skirt ensemble always speaks to a Mary Jane girl. Quintessentially neat and crisply dressed, your jewelry should be pearls: coordinated necklace and earrings (given to you for your twelfth birthday by your mom) and an antique pearl ring from your grandma adorning your right pinkie finger. Hair swept back in a ponytail, often with a ribbon, and brushed at all times. Makeup is simple and traditional: lipstick in a color that matches a handbag or shoes, and neat, clean foundation with a touch of rose in the cheeks.

📱 work it, girl

It is important that your skills are appreciated and you are given plenty of positive recognition. You will bloom and beam in these sorts of conditions. You will be happy using your detail skills at a local library, reorganizing the reference section, or working as an antique furniture restorer. As a high-powered executive assistant, successfully managing a very irascible boss with big business demands, your calm and soothing manner, along with your cool thinking and problem solving, would come into play.

💘 finding a sole mate

A mate who opens doors and sends regular doses of fresh flowers (accompanied by a sweet note, of course) is the perfect match for you. Lawyers can be an excellent match as you appreciate their logic and rhetoric. And since they often find you the perfect companion, for you are perky, witty, and extremely considerate, this is a good combination. Other possible pairings include classical musicians, provided they are not too serious, and woodworkers.

INVOKING YOUR INNER STILETTO

Donning a pair of racy, sheer boy-shorts underneath your skirt is the perfect way to harness your feminine wiles - they'll accentuate the plump roundness of your pink cheeks in a nice way that only you'll know about!

famous

MARY JANE GIRLS

KATE SPADE, MOLLY SHANNON,
TWIGGY, EMMA THOMPSON

CLOG

The Clog girl moves with a feeling of solidity under her feet. No matter how hectic or chaotic things are, you are sure about where you are going and what you are going to attain. Your vibe is mellow, but don't mistake it for lazy. You are extremely hardworking and possess a deep spirituality, either consciously or unconsciously, which gives everything you do a sort of gravitas. Never giddy or overly excited, your natural state is an easy balance with not too many high highs or low lows.

★ completing the look

You'll be happiest in clothing you can move in; a printed flowing skirt or painters pants in khaki, denim, or faded dark red work well. Cotton boat-neck tees or tanks in neutral colors top off the outfit. Whatever the length, keep your hair off your face with a printed bandanna or simple hair tie, and keep the makeup to a minimum with a sheer peach lip gloss, just for enhancement, and a simple natural moisturizer for the face.

📱 work it, girl

If you are a Clog girl, it is important for you to feel that you are contributing to the earth somehow in your work. A food co-op, an environmental outfit, a chef at an all-natural restaurant, and an organic farmer are all good ways to benefit the earth and work well with your natural groundedness.

💘 finding a sole mate

Finding mates who are as down-to-earth as you are, are true to themselves, and have a distinctly mellow vibe is important. A Clog girl is never happy with someone who is disingenuous. A natural flow of loving feeling to and from your mate is essential, rather than any wild proclamations of love or, on the contrary, contentious lovers' spats. Consistency and smoothness is the key here.

INVOKING YOUR INNER STILETTO

Turn your groundedness on it's head and do something absolutely and completely silly: jump on a trampoline, get your hair blown out for no reason at all, or give in to your temptation to wear a very bold red lipstick.

RETRO BASKETBALL

Quiet and shy, you are a real dreamer. Creatively blessed, you can just look at a piece of paper and an amazing design will practically appear. You love to read avant-garde glossy magazines, fascinated with the layout, graphics, and pictures, and you have a very defined and particular aesthetic when it comes to your own work. You probably went to a small liberal arts college where you majored in fine arts. You are not a huge socializer, but because you are always one of the coolest cats of the bunch, you are frequently invited to the hottest events. Quiet and a bit indrawn, you can be very shy, but when you look out from those long lashes, you treat others to a kind and inquisitive attention.

completing the look

Definitely an individual, you look best in jeans by an up-and-coming edgy designer, preferably that drag a bit on the ground for a cool ragged-edge effect and a vintage blazer, distressed and a little ripped up, over a custom tee, all in dark hues of black, eggplant, purple, or olive. Your hair is cut in fringy bangs, which cover your eyes a bit, and makeup is minimalist but dramatic — kohl eyeliner, lots of mascara, pale complexion, and a hint of light pink lip gloss all work well to keep the cool effects going.

 ## work it, girl

Your dreamy creativeness means that a career in fine art or high fashion suits you well. Though your behind-the-scenes aesthetic make an important impression on the world at large, you yourself are rarely seen in the public eye, choosing to pursue your calling in the background, where your ideas can flourish.

finding a sole mate

Your mates have got to be independent thinkers, a little punky, with an appreciation for the *Ramones*. Their aesthetics have got to cross over into yours and even match at times in order for you to groove together. You shouldn't even entertain the idea of someone in the business world, instead going for the bassist in the latest electroclash band, graphic designer, or even journalist (though not one in the immediate media glare). A sense of humor is important, for you can tend to be a little melancholy. A partner who can gently lift you with a little joke or two is always beneficial for you.

INVOKING YOUR INNER STILETTO

Slash a deeper V in that vintage tee of yours and try a dark smokey maroon nail polis on your nails. Sex and sass!

Chapter three

ON-THE-GO

*One word: active. In whatever you do,
be it athletic endeavors, purposeful walking
to and from work, or nights out, you ladies
approach life with determination and zeal.
You are health conscious - life always
includes a walk across town or a daily run.
You like to know you are covering ground,
even if it is only to t he grocery store
and back. Extremely independent,you tend
to have love affairs based on mutual
admiration and fun activities.*

POINTY TOE SKIMMER

Oh, you are smart, aren't you? And pert, too. Whipping around the office, making sure all p's and q's are taken care of. You might be getting your boss's coffee, with your pad of To Do's in hand, crossing each one off in perfect harmony with your rhythmic morning office survey, or making sure your desk drawers are in perfect order. The absolutely charming thing about you is that however together you might appear, you've always got a little something tripping up your image. Getting your skirt stuck on a file cabinet while you are diligently filing, falling off your chair unexpectedly in the middle of a dinner date, tripping into your boss's arms in the elevator. Rather than being entirely flummoxed, you manage it with a sweet innocent charm, always pausing to tuck your hair back behind your ear after each incident and going back to whatever task is at hand, with studied determination.

⭐ completing the look

Easy A-line skirts in a viscose/cotton blend, structured blouses, and feminine jackets nipped at the waist are all good choices for you. A careful reference to the 1960s with a modern update and high-quality materials with a touch of luxury — think a mink-trimmed cardigan sweater, for instance — further enhance your natural charms. Hair in a perky bob held back with a jeweled barrette and pink and red lipsticks always complement your look nicely.

📱 work it, girl

You've got to be in an office. You are the one who adds a bit of glamour and style to the place as well as keeping it in thrumming and humming order, as if it ran by itself. Good fields to land in are real estate (you'd be the COO after working your way up from agent), a law firm (working your way to managing partner after being a legal assistant), and investment banking (you'd be the right-hand woman to the CEO) or even working in an architectural firm as an engineer.

🐾 finding a sole mate

With classic good looks and athletic and rugged in some ways, your mate has got to be a perfect blend of proper upbringing and unruffled attitude about your many careening episodes. In fact, your mate has to find your episodes completely and totally lovable — finding them the most charming thing about you!

INVOKING YOUR INNER STILETTO

You know what? I think a black lace garter belt, sans panties, underneath your skirt will really have you feeling your femininity nicely.

LOAFER

From the classic penny loafer to the modified modern loafer, loafers signify an American ease, classic styling, and practicality that always envelop the girl who wears them. Whether you're donning a cordovan classic or a molded rubber-heel Italian version, most of you are the essence of common sense. Speedily working things to a satisfying conclusion, you are not afraid to get right into the mix of whatever is going on, be it a business deal or family spat. You lend a mix of good cheer and humor, a down-to-earth perspective, and a commitment to a resolution that suits everyone involved. You are a great best friend to have, a wise counselor who is always up for a bit of fun and are energetic about helping solve your pals' problems just as fast as you solve your own.

⭐ completing the look

Make sure you have a fine-weave thin dress sock to wear with your loafer, whatever type it may be. Pants in a solid color, usually black, that are neat, creased, and have a slim-tailored fit and a bit of stretch for easy movement are key. For maximum loafer effect, pants should hang with a slight fold below the ankle, just covering the middle of the shoe nicely. A crisp blouse, with just a bit of starch, in an eggshell blue or white is an appropriate pairing, a slim jacket for day, and for evening a silk cardigan sweater in black work well with the pants. If a skirt is desired, try pleated, just above the knee, and a solid-color opaque tight. Hair is neat, a short bob tucked behind the ears or neatly back in a ponytail where nary a wisp escapes. Makeup is a touch of a rosy blush, mascara, and a light pink gloss.

📱 work it, girl

Honestly, if you're a Loafer girl, you are going to do well anywhere you land. Try for a place where your hard work will have a high payoff — an investment bank or a nonprofit you really believe in, because any organization that is lucky to have you will benefit from your enormous drive, diplomacy, and ever-positive willingness to get the job done.

finding a sole mate

You want someone who is just as adept at navigating the world as you are, but it's good if your mates have a knack for silliness as well. This way, they can always be counted on for a bit of fun when you are in the thick of things — an important way for some of your intensity to lessen. Consistency and sense of purpose are key — a mate who knows what life is all about, beyond work and getting things done.

INVOKING YOUR INNER STILETTO

I want to see you throw purpose to the wind; do something wild just for the sake of wildness, whether it be breaking out into a little salsa dance, putting on some sexy undies, or even just taking different way to work. Whatever it is it has to have no purpose at all!

SNEAKER

The Sneaker girl is all about cool, but very accessible cool. Normally seen dashing about town, you always know the coolest music and films. You are quick on your feet and witty, often peppering your conversation with a bit of ironic or sarcastic humor just for effect. And then you're gone just as fast as you arrived.

⭐ completing the look

Try flared-leg fine-wale cords in solid bold colors: pumpkin, eggplant, hunter green, or black. A vintage or customized tee under a long-sleeved button-down, also of vintage descent, completes the look. Hair should be totally natural in whatever form it may take - short spiky and a bit punky, or long and curly. Only makeup that can be applied while in dashing mode will do - lip gloss from a tube, tinted moisturizer with sunscreen, and mascara usually work well. Accoutrements are more often something handmade and rustic - a rope necklace with handmade bead, a sturdy backpack or messenger bag in a bright color that is a bit distressed from constant use.

📱 work it, girl

You have got to be producing something to be happy: film, music, cool lifestyle magazine - whatever it is, it's got to be hipster and zippy. Constant motion is the only state you'll be happy in, so find a place that requires much of you in the way of shepherding ideas, film canisters, edits, or photography from one place to another, along with your expertise in behind-the-scenes running.

🧍 finding a sole mate

You want someone who will go skateboarding and exploring with you, just as easily as hanging at home on a Saturday afternoon, chilling and listening to the latest French house CD. Your mates have got to be flexible, fun, and actually get your ironic remarks. A little bit of a thick skin helps so that they never get hurt by your ironies, but not too thick. They've got to be able to open up emotionally and listen to your dreams and desires just as well. It's important for a Sneaker girl to feel she always has a place of safe, sweet loving with her mate where she can really open up and lose her freneticism.

INVOKING YOUR INNER STILETTO

*Showing off your creamy
shoulders can be a nice touch.
What about a light pink or deep plum
tank of mercerized cotton with lacy trim
to pair with your cords?
Add some dangly earrings. Voila!*

RUNNING SHOE

You are recognizable by your very purposeful walk. Outwardly friendly yet also brusque and businesslike, you seem to be extremely buoyant and at the same time very directed in all of your goings to and fro.

Whether you're getting your business-school degree or just going to work out, you are streaming through life with a walk that is grounded. You usually believe that there is nothing in life a little determination and hard work won't solve. Through this lens you view most of life's situations, which can be both extraordinarily uplifting and frustrating to those around you, as you can dole out tactical support with the best of them but can't really understand why someone would ever need an extended crying jag.

⭐ completing the look

Complete the look with a pair of khakis and a high-quality cotton tee. You don't want anything to interfere with your freedom of movement or air of purposefulness. To appear neat, approachable, and hardworking at all times, your hair is either in a bob or a neat ponytail; either way it is all one length - no layers.

Wear your college ring and a string of pearls. Because you wear pretty serious running shoes, it always seems like you are leaning in a little bit, like a runner getting ready for a sprint. And in some ways you are, since you are always getting ready for the next challenge life is handing you. Light pink lip gloss and a touch of rosy blush complete your energetic look.

📱 work it, girl

If you are not a world-class athlete yourself, you are running a global, market-making corporation.

finding a sole mate

You'll easily find your Sole Mate while you are out running one day. Your mate will respond to your sense of purpose and your natural cheery demeanor. You need someone who will be able to run the marathons of life with you, a cheerleader and a steady confidant.

INVOKING YOUR INNER STILETTO

A nice way to do this is slowing your run all the way down to a walk. Get into the present moment and make each step a slow, gliding, feminine, seductive movement.

famous

RUNNING SHOE GIRLS

JACKIE JOYNER-KERSEE,
MARY LOU RETTON,
BRANDI CHASTAIN

OXFORD WINGTIP

You are deeply individualistic and are very comfortable in your own skin. Not afraid to mix up the masculine and feminine in your style, you take your time and make decisions based on what fits for you, for your life, and you are not to be swayed by any outside sources or opinions. You tend towards seriousness in your endeavors and your everyday, and take an observational approach to life. You might be found at the helm of a downtown arts magazine you founded yourself, or you might be a visual artist mixing up mediums in the studio. You tend toward the experimental and the modern with an eye for groundbreaking ideas. You tend toward the solitary, creating things on your own and then managing them from a distance as you launch them into the world. You appreciate irony and you never judge it, but incorporate it into your work, noticing and embracing life's paradoxes with an observant eye. You don't tend to be snarky, but you fall on the spectrum of more of a dry humor than silly gigglyness.

★ completing the look

You are about quality and timelessness. Make sure the button downs you wear are well made, and beautifully constructed. Tap into your inner junior high school girl by pairing your oxford wingtips with a knee length or longer skirt. Tailored wide-legged trousers and a jacket create a polished effect, or skinny jeans and fitted simple white t-shirt amplify your inner rockabilly. Mix it up with a floppy hat, or some tortoiseshell combs in your hair to keep the tresses aside. Makeup is simple with a statement eye or lip - think kohl rimmed eyes or a deep red hue on the lips - but not both.

work it, girl

Oxford wingtip girls do well in fields that require steady determination, patience and creativity. Founder of a literary magazine, architect, visual artist creating large sculptural work, a modern librarian or graphic designer at a downtown magazine. Any vocation that lets you be creative behind the scenes, constructing, observing, is a good fit for you. The world of fashion can be a good place to lend your skills because your natural level of detachment allows for you to discover timeless talent without getting caught up in trends.

finding a sole mate

You need a mate who draws out your feminine side, someone who can appreciate your innate eccentricities and creative nature, who won't try to reign you in. Your partner has got to be one to gently tease that sense of ironic humor you have lurking inside and be strong enough to take any sarcasm that might be thrown their way. They should be open to new ideas and a modern, forward thinking person who appreciates the new and embraces the classic.

INVOKING YOUR INNER STILETTO

Invest in the ultimate pair of luxury oxford wingtips, custom-made in Italy, shined to a glorious sheen to bring out the inner stiletto in you.

WORKINGMAN'S BOOT

You may be kicking someone's ass at the moment, metaphorically, of course. At the very least, you are probably standing up for yourself, reading someone the riot act, or kicking in the fender of the taxi that just tried to overcharge you.

Your inner spirit is sometimes more in sync with volcanoes than any other type of shoe girl. You are prone to explosion, but this is good, because you assist society and culture by constantly agitating and forcing people to reexamine their own behavior. We dearly need you to keep things lively - that's for sure.

A Workingman's Boot girl customarily believes that agitation is the spice of life. Most happy when things are really cooking, swinging, and generally happening, you often find yourself in the middle of cultural movements, mosh pits, and PTA uprisings. Fortunately, your sense of fear is minimal, and your ease in these situations is high. Not always the leader of these movements, you are sometimes the volatile sidekick, inspiring everyone to take action with your rousing words that follow (or occur during) the headliner's speech. To be comfortable with you is to be comfortable with the fact that any given situation is rich ground for dissent.

★ completing the look

It is important for you to be fully expressed in your wardrobe, hair, and makeup. Hair looks great spiky, and color is an important element for a WB girl. Body art usually figures prominently; it is important for you to feel that your body is a true expression of your beliefs and causes. Try looks that allow for martial art kicks when needed - baggy black parachute pants, a pleated mini with distressed black tights, and a leather coat so that you can feel protected. If you are of the fully butching-it variety, a white tee, denim overalls, and a large swagger help you feel fully in your Workingman's Boot element.

📱 work it, girl

While a coffeehouse may seem like an odd place for you to land, it is often a good place for you. You have free java to keep you wired, an ear to a lot of different movements in the community, and a flexible work schedule, which is great since going to see bands play in the evening is a major part of your happiness. That is, if you're not playing in the band, which is another great occupation for you. Getting your screeching guitar and heavy drum on in a serious downtown garage rock band or fronting the latest angry female hit machine is a wonderful way for you to express yourself - and support yourself, to boot.

🐾 finding a sole mate

Loyalty is the No. 1 recommended trait for you to feel happy and secure in a relationship. Because you find yourself in a higher number than average of altercations, physical strength is another, as you want to know that when looking out for your back, your mate can also go to bat for you in a pinch. An exception to this is the butch lady. You, on the contrary, are better matched with someone petite, feminine, and in a flouncy miniskirt.

INVOKING YOUR INNER STILETTO

*Get in touch with your softer side
by taking it down a notch.
When tempted to scrap, see how
it feels not to react, just for a moment.*

famous

WORKINGMAN'S BOOT GIRLS

PINK ,AVRIL LAVIGNE,
ANI DIFRANCO,
JANEANE GAROFALO

HIKING BOOT

You are intrepid. You have no problem hiking over a mountain, stream, glacier, or other natural creation. You move with assuredness through life, often intuiting what the next right step is before you make it. After years of adventures, you've learned to trust yourself, and your air of quiet confidence is unshakable. Having faced many of nature's absurdities, you've got a hilarious sense of humor and a built-in hardiness that can withstand even the most grueling of conditions. But make no mistake, you also possess a very feminine allure, that of the woman-adventurer, a free spirit who knows the value of her own footstep.

⭐ completing the look

Get into warm, flexible fleece pants, treated with waterproofing, that tuck easily into your boots or adjust with a pulley. Zip-up fleeces and turtlenecks in bright colors are only one of the many layers that are advantageous for you to wear. Hair is either cropped short or long and tied back in a ponytail. Makeup tends to be a waterproof sunscreen of high SPF, lip protectant, and a natural glowing radiance that comes from being active and outdoors. You may have the odd bit of whimsy, a fun necklace from one of the many tribes you've met, a charm on your fleece zipper from home, even a tattoo or two.

📱 work it, girl

You've got to be outside and using your body and hands to be happy. Working as a biologist in the field, an anthropologist studying tribal cultures, an archaeologist digging up the latest Egyptian tomb, a navigator of snow caves, or a National Geographic producer are all excellent matches for you.

🐾 finding a sole mate

It's best if your mate is in the same field as you so that coordinating together time is a minimum hassle. Plus, it's good for you to work side by side with your mate; there's nothing better for your spirit than to be in your element and have the one you love along for the ride. Your mate's got to be able to roll with the punches nature throws at you two together and laugh along with you just as heartily.

INVOKING YOUR INNER STILETTO

*Replace your laces with big
satin ribbons and tie them in a large
floppy bow. The wideness of the
ribbon will ensure that they last
through your next jungle adventure,
and the satin will remind you
of your feminine side as you
conquer the elements.*

COWBOY BOOT

You could be an actual cowgirl on the prairie or a city girl with a cowgirl heart. Either way, you've got a zing about you, a little extra panache that comes from inherent confidence. You probably know how to rope a steer or head up a multimillion-dollar film. With an intensity that runs deep, your penetrating eyes get to the bottom of things, even in the most casual conversation.

★ completing the look

The No. 1 wardrobe essential for you should be jeans. Slim-fitting, to the waist, dark or faded, and easy to move in. A long, flowing skirt is a close second. For the city girl, a bit of glitz on the top is always a perfect complement: maybe a customized tee with lacy accoutrement. For the girl on the range, a typical cowboy shirt works well, with some feminine braiding. Hair in a ponytail is helpful, even if it is wisping out just a bit, since you could be herding cattle or engineering a movie shoot, but it's better that it not get in the way of the major project at hand.

📱 work it, girl

Straight-shooting work is best. A Cowboy Boot girl should not be assigned any extraneous tasks, only projects that let you get your hands dirty, roll up your sleeves, and start kicking. Whether film director or chef or ranch owner, all CB girls have one thing in common workwise, and that is you like getting the job done.

👢 finding a sole mate

Interestingly, you are actually rather private. A good Sole Mate match for you is someone who is a bit quiet when it comes to matters of the heart, who will appreciate you for your energy but not be overly demonstrative. It is imperative that your mate be a solid partner and a gentle comfort and support to you when your hard-drivin' day is done.

INVOKING YOUR INNER STILETTO

*Swap your jeans out for a skirt—
there's nothing sexier than boots
and a skirt: just a hint of calf,
a whisper of thigh, but still a hard-
drivin' attitude!*

KNEE-HIGH BOOT
WITH LOW HEEL

As on-the-go as all the other girls, you are very dedicated to looking sleek as you zoom from place to place. You favor a black boot, with a molded rubber or stacked wood heel, made from a fine leather. The knee high boot with low heel gives you added flair as you have a tendency to wear it with skirts, thus giving a bit of a sassy vibe to your comings and goings. You are a fount of common sense, always at the ready with a hearty laugh or a bit of practical advice. You know how to change a tire on a car, but if you're with a man, you'll let him do it just to make him feel like a hero.

★ completing the look

For your days zipping about town, try bootleg slim-fit jeans with a solid color tee and a corduroy jacket. For evening events, a just-below-the-knee A-line skirt works well with a slim turtle-neck sweater - thick-ply cashmere, of course, or a pretty embroidered tank and a denim jacket. Makeup is simple and clean - no fuss, lip gloss, sheer color on the cheeks, and a bit of mascara; in the evenings, a tiny hint o f sparkle around the eyes brings out your playfulness. Jewelry is classic: pearl or diamond studs.

work it, girl

You've got to be in an artistic pursuit to be happy. Whether this means you are a writer, visual artist, sculptor, or musician, or work for any of the above, you've got to have your hand in some creative place to feel fully alive.

finding a sole mate

Your mates have got to have a jolly side to them. A mate who is too buttoned up will simply not work with you, because for all your practicality, you like to have a lot of fun in everyday life. A mate with solid middle-class values and a steady job is always beneficial since your income might be a bit chaotic.

INVOKING YOUR INNER STILETTO

I want to see some crocheted tights in a dark purple under your A-line skirt. Just a peek of the knee in these, you'll be feeling your inner stiletto in no time.

Chapter four

TOWERING HEIGHTS

Towering Heights Girls love your heels.
You adore the click of your sound on the pavement,
the arch they create in your foot,
the slight sway they create in your walk,
the lengthening of the leg, the slimming
of the silhouette, the headiness of the view
from up there. You love your air
a little thinner. On the whole, you tend to
be a bit more involved in their appearance
and are always very interested in presenting
a carefully prepared persona. You are more
given to passionate love affairs and fall
in love easily. And you, more than the other
fundamental shoe girls, like to dress up
on an everyday basis.

CLASSIC CONSERVATIVE PUMP

You may be diligently scanning the Financial Times and Wall Street Journal on your way to work at an investment bank, an accounting firm, or a law firm. You most likely have a cup of coffee in one hand, the paper in another, and an overstuffed laptop bag. Appearing a bit discombobulated, you are actually simultaneously reading the paper, scanning your text messages, drinking your coffee, and jotting a note for your morning meeting in your PDA.

You are a most loyal friend, unflagging in your ability to show up for any event, any time of day, always available for a quick joke and a laugh. Extraordinarily good-natured and extremely resilient, you've got a man's fraternité and affability, making you a most valued friend since you are always so easygoing. Smart as a whip, you can rattle off stock indexes as easily as the latest baseball scores without missing a beat. You can work until 4 a.m., be in the office at 8 a.m., and still make it to your best friend's birthday party that evening with a smile on your face and the perfect present in your hands. Your values are basic: work hard, get paid well, use your brain, value your family and friends, and give back. You are not overly cheery in bad situations, but rather rock solid and consistently pleasant.

completing the look

Five or six interchangeable navy and black suits, one with a pinstripe (plus a few light-khaki linen ones thrown in for summer), are neat, easy looks for you. Because ease of movement is essential, wearing pants with your jackets and a simple blouse or a fine-weave cashmere sweater work best. Jewelry is minimal - a pair of pearls or diamond studs, a school ring, and a necklace from your sweet sixteen work. Best if your hair is kept back during the workday and out of fussing range. Lip gloss is all you need - your complexion is usually very good and always has a natural bit of rosy glow.

 ## work it, girl

A law firm, accounting firm, or investment bank are good choices, that is, if you are not president of your own media company or a CEO already. You worked your tail off in school, Ivy League, summa cum laude, and were involved in multiple extracurricular clubs, including fundraising and tutoring for underprivileged children.

 ## finding a sole mate

You need the same great qualities that make you a standout: constant, resilient, good-natured, and fun. Fortunately, you assume this is what everyone is like and because you never lower your standards, you've always got an adoring mate and loads of friends.

INVOKING YOUR INNER STILETTO

Try lollygagging in a lounge chair for a few minutes, and get a little Vitamin D from the sun - just a few minutes worth is good for your whole metabolism.

T-STRAP

Ta-daaaa! A T-Strap girl always arrives with a bit of a splash. You are either in your latest Broadway musical or just taking the everyday office water-cooler talk up a notch. Always a bit peppier than those around you, you have a penchant for launching into a show tune, which has everyone else laughing and singing along. If they don't know the words, you'll give a quick, good-natured lesson. Others can't really help but be infected by your natural gutsiness and Betty Boop—like cuteness. You often look like you stepped off the set of a '40s movie, steno pad in hand.

★ completing the look

T-Strap girls always look good in a slim, structured skirt and a neatly tucked-in cotton blouse for a daytime office gig. In the evening, a pair of fishnets adds a bit of theatricality and fun, paired with a slim skirt and simple boatneck top in black jersey for ease of movement.

📱 work it, girl

If you are not actually living in your T-straps for your latest gig on Broadway, you do best in an office where you can showcase your natural showwomanship and be appreciated for your virtues. A film company is always a good match, and any studio would be lucky to have you — you can easily manage a chaotic environment with your good nature and penchant for song. Your unique ability to manage up (with little or no knowledge on the part of those being managed) always adds a sweet hum to any environment, turning any place you land into a well-oiled machine.

💘 finding a sole mate

This lady needs a song mate, one who will whistle a tune from 42nd Street under his breath and look quizzically up at you, daring you to name the tune on the spot. Your playfulness needs to be matched in pure fun — a bump on a log or shrinking violet is not for you.

INVOKING YOUR INNER STILETTO

*Show off some showstopping gams
with some backseam stocking.
Me-OW!*

OPEN TOE

Getting on your boyfriend's Vespa just outside a hip café in the coolest part of town, you are averse to a helmet since it will mess with your carefully coiffed '40s updo with cute bangs. You might be zipping off to a gig where a mix of vintage jazz and modern doo-wop is the main attraction. Or maybe you are in your 1965 Cadillac convertible on your way to the flea market. Wherever you are off to, you usually make a sassy entrance with your shiny open-toe heels that tilt you just a little forward, put an extra zing in your walk, and give onlookers a tiny peek of the toe cleavage.

★ completing the look

Skirts, mostly in the "New Look" style, full and waist-accentuating, show off your natural flair. Shirtwaists should figure prominently, veering toward a more classic '60s silhouette. If you're a curvaceous gal, you should accentuate your figure. If you're not entirely buxom, accenting the curviest parts of your body with a little dart and a tuck is perfect. With jeans, the bottoms should be rolled up, shirt elegantly tied around your waist. Lipstick should always be in a darker shade of red or violet and always be applied. (An Open-Toe Shoe girl with naked lips is not recommended.)

📱 work it, girl

As an Open-Toe girl, you do best in an extremely detail-oriented and artistic career. Naturally very discerning about your occupation, careers as a vintage eyeglass or art restorer, upholsterer, or wallpaper designer are all good matches for you. Since you are extremely practical in all matters of business, you excel at owning your own business and are often renowned in your aesthetic circles for your work.

🦋 finding a sole mate

You will do well with mates who are appreciative of the fine arts. They've got to be able to hang at a museum as well as the local jazz bar. You also work well with mates who are good with their hands: carpenters, wrought-iron workers, and sculptors are good matches for you.

INVOKING YOUR INNER STILETTO

A silk halter top shows off your gorgeous arms and shoulders. Make sure the halter ties in a cheeky little bow at the back of the neck for extra Stiletto.

KNEE-HIGH BOOT
WITH HIGH HEEL

A Knee-High Boot with High-Heel girl is most likely committed to the life of the bourgeoisie; middle-class values to you are the true essence of life. Education is highly prized, and you are well read, kind to all you encounter, a solid citizen, and a rock-solid foundation to your family and friends. Your sense of humor is unflappable; you value hard work and believe in regular holidays and the importance of being neatly turned out at all times. You have three or four pairs of black high-heel knee-high boots that you get cleaned, resoled, and repaired every spring. When one pair finally reaches the end of its sometimes fifteen-year run, you carefully hit the first fall sale to replace it.

★ completing the look

You favor classic looks — and you should. Your shoes reveal your inherent classic taste in everything from music to furniture, and your looks are often representative of that as well. Tailored slacks with a merino wool tiny cabled twin set in a bright color and your hair neatly arranged in a bob or pulled pack in a neat ponytail are good looks for you. For evening, a long skirt with a slit in front up to the knee, showing off your boots, paired with a silk top in a jewel tone or evening jacket works best.

📱 work it, girl

You work well in professions that are structured and perceived as steady and prestigious. Banking is a good fit for you, though most likely you'll fit better in the marketing department than on a trading floor. You're the one who communicates the best with senior management and CEOs; as a consequence, you usually rise to a top position at whatever firm you land at.

💘 finding a sole mate

Trusty is the No. 1 trait you should look for in a mate. Your heart needs to know your mate is always there for you through the good and the bad, for celebrating the joys of life with you and being a solid presence in your life. Consistency is a key trait, and you deserve a mate with this quality for it is one of your own shining virtues.

INVOKING YOUR INNER STILETTO

Try a boot with a wild design, one with unusual textures like python or snake - or even one with bold colored patterns and cutwork - scalloped edging, contrasting stitching, or metallic heels. Yeah, baby!

ANKLE BOOT WITH HIGH HEEL

You may be stepping out of a sleek black hired car in the city or lunching at a top restaurant. You are definitely both accustomed to luxury and fully in the mix of the latest social goings-on. You can slice and dice a business deal in two shakes of your pony-skin bag and at the same time negotiate your two-year-old and five-year-old's spat of the moment with an earthy intuition. You are matter-of-fact feminine, at ease in your skin and your abilities.

completing the look

Recommended gear for this girl are tight-fitting jeans and a slim cashmere sweater for day, and for evening, jeans or slim-fitting satin pants paired with a sparkly top. Your hair is usually best worn down and framing the face, with neutral makeup; a mauve-tinted lipstick or even a neutral lip work well for you. This combination of body-hugging clothes and careful makeup gives you an added edge - you are no doubt one of the most feminine creatures others have ever encountered; yet you are no-nonsense and down-to-earth at the same time.

work it, girl

You have a special talent for getting things done in a very frank and open way. You are just as straightforward in any kind of business dealing and are always in the mood to strike a bargain. For this reason, you are happiest in professions that require a lot of wheeling and dealing and relationship skills. Real estate is an excellent choice for you, as well as owning a modeling agency, construction company, gen-eral contracting company, or even a sports team.

🦁 *finding a sole mate*

You need a mate who will take care of you, who will navigate the city streets to make sure you don't snag your heel in a hole or get thrown off balance. Your mate has to like luxury and spoil you with all the trappings a woman like you desires; this will be rewarded by a happy woman, as devoted and loyal as a lioness toward her cubs.

INVOKING YOUR INNER STILETTO

*Try some just-kissed red lipstick-
go for the shade your lips would be
had you just engaged in a lusty
makeout session.*

MULE WITH HIGH HEEL

You are most often found in a sunny climate, preferring the summer season to all others. Most likely, you've just served a guest a fruity pink drink from a pink tray and are now sitting down next to your guest, poolside, with a copy of Cosmopolitan in your hand, just for fun. More often than not, you are the hostess of whatever summertime poolside gathering all your girlfriends are attending, whether it be a just-for-two spa lunch or a full-on barbecue.

★ completing the look

Pink and lime-green capri pants in a Palm Beach print, paired with a white shirtwaist. Slim, black, cotton capri pants are a close second, paired with a red-and-white-striped boatneck with three-quarter sleeves. In the evening, the capri pant is paired with a taffeta or silk shell and pearls. Hair is in a ponytail, and sunglasses are a must-have accessory, no matter what time of day. Any skirt should be short and straight – no flounces.

📱 work it, girl

You typically excel at any position in the decorative arts. From working in interior design to wardrobe consultation to flower arranging, you add a flair to anything you put your hands on and are most happy when making something more beautiful.

💘 finding a sole mate

Your mate has got to be above average in looks and well groomed. You must be able to link arms with your mate down the street and feel that together, you make a beautiful couple.

INVOKING YOUR INNER STILETTO

Take yourself up another notch and try a little platform in that high heel mule, see how high you can go and how it feels from up where you are!

HIGH-HEEL SANDAL

The woman who finds herself in high-heel sandals for a majority of her shoe time is a woman who is very confident in her femininity. Toes are most likely always pedicured perfectly in coral or pink. Your ability to balance a cocktail tray, glass of wine, piece of hardware or two, soccer ball, and the odd child or two in both hands, while glowing with feminine wiles, is a testament to your balancing prowess in all matters of life, your determination, and your extremely strong ab muscles. You are a woman who has the very special ability to make things just a little more festive than they were before you arrived, a quality much needed in this world.

★ *completing the look*

You look best in very feminine colors and fabrics - light and dark pinks, taffetas, silks, white, corals. Tailored pants, often capri-style to show off the ankle, or very short skirts work well for the High-Heel Sandal girl. Looks are best as simple and classic, not frilly, and always with a distinct accoutrement - a lovely pin, a ribbon or two, a charm bracelet dangling fetchingly from your wrist.

work it, girl

The most important quality for your work is that it actively engage you. Whether you are a mom, an interior designer, a general contractor, a professional organizer, or a real estate maven, you've got to be consistently moving from one project to the next in order to keep yourself in tip-top shape.

finding a sole mate

You need someone cozy to cozy up to, someone who adores you and appreciates your femininity in every single one of its forms. You like to be taken care of and also like to take care of your mates, spoiling them from time to time with surprise gifts and always lots of love.

INVOKING YOUR INNER STILETTO

*Already embracing your power
of height, go for a sandal
with some straps and beading, paired
with a slightly shorter skirt than you
normally would. Lovely.*

PLATFORM SHOE

People definitely hear you before they see you. You are not afraid of making noise that is for sure. Your shoes actually lead the way, hitting the floor with a definitive impact from the extra added weight in the toe box. But you prefer the noise and the higher the better; the view from up top is one you really, really like. You are not afraid to take chances and will risk an occasional fall or tumble just to keep cruising the world at a different altitude. You get cabs very easily in your elevated status and you are willing to experiment with ensembles from many different eras from 1920s to 1970s and everything in between. You understand that platforms are anthropologically speaking more trendy when there is chaos in the world, but to you they are essential everyday.

★ *completing the look*

You have got it together that is for sure. Whatever platform of the day you are wearing whether it be a giant clunky wedge or a platform stiletto, it is all about inhabiting the entire feeling ot platform; big, loud and brash. Skinny jeans and sparkly tops, mini-skirts, maxi dresses with bold prints, make up can be simple or very dramatic - dark kohl eyes are common among platform girls. Hair is usually left pretty wild or completely and perfectly blown out.

work it, girl

You like to be in the action. It might be a Vegas boxing ring and you are the ring girl, it might be front row at a couture collection fashion show, it might be running PR at a major film studio, or doing a major new exhibit at your art gallery - if things are percolating, you are there!

🐎 *finding a sole mate*

Look for a mate who is ok with you towering above them every once in awhile - or even all the time. They have got to be very confident in their own skin, and you could use a mate who is a little more mellow than you are, someone who doesn't mind being the grounding influence on the party. Also, they have got to be willing to lend an arm when crossing any streets.

INVOKING YOUR INNER STILETTO

You are already way up high, looking down, so invoke your inner stiletto by investing in a gorgeous pair of earrings that highlight the color of your eyes to bring attention to your face and balance out all that excitement going on down below.

STILETTO

You move through the world with an uber-confident horsey walk and are often found on a city street, hailing a cab while talking on your phone. An intriguing mix of traditional and modern, deep down you believe in the fact that men provide and women look good. At the same time, you embrace your raw female power, stepping out smartly, never afraid to state what you want. You are extremely self-possessed and very much your own woman.

★ *completing the look*

You work your shoe into most any look with ease, well aware of its leg-lengthening, streamlining advantages. Try tailored jeans and a customized tee on a weekend day or a vampy, '40s-era, black straight-skirted dress for evening cocktails (emphasizing a tiny bit of the S&M properties inherent in a pair of towering black stilettos). At work, an A-line slim-fitting skirt and matching jacket with slim streamlined lapels and neatly tucked-in blouse work well. Makeup is precise and should include a darker shade of lipstick - either red or violet - worn regardless of season or trend. Hair is immaculately trimmed and often tied back in an elegant ponytail or neatly brushed and is always shiny.

📱 *work it, girl*

Your natural self-confidence means you'll make a great entertainment executive, performer, owner of a PR firm, or editor in chief at a major fashion magazine. Your shoes establish you as an alpha-female even before you begin to speak. There is no doubt who runs things when you arrive on the scene.

🦁 *finding a sole mate*

Power, elegance, and self-possession. That's really it.

INVOKING YOUR INNER STILETTO

Keep on your Stilettos, take off all your clothes, stand in front of your mirror, and let yourself know how truly gorgeous you are.

famous

STILETTO GIRLS

MARILYN MONROE, ANNA WINTOUR,
SARAH JESSICA PARKER,
BETTY PAIGE, HEDWIG, BEYONCÉ

ADDENDUM

custom-made shoes A favorite topic of mine: custom-made, or couture, shoes. These of course are shoes made specifically for your feet only. Can you imagine! The sheer opulence of it. Trust me, it is truly divine. Typically, a shoemaker who specializes in custom work will take detailed measurements of your feet, let you select your style and materials, and voilà! Custom-made shoes feel like ecstatic slippers on your feet - they fit like a glove and since the materials are of an extremely high grade, they will mold to your feet as you wear them, creating a fit like no other. Pure luxury.

getting a leg up No matter what your Shoe sign, putting your delicate foot into a sumptuous stocking (knee- or thigh-high) can bring a pinch of stiletto to any ensemble. Try fishnets in black or deep eggplant or herringbone cutwork patterns, jacquards or lace, crocheted or ribbed textures, sensual and plush all-cashmere.

accessorize me! Your shoes need accessories, too. Satin ribbons, clip-on jewels, feather puffs, ostrich plumes, a delicate chain or two, even silk handmade flowers. Any of these are easy to find and quickly take it up a notch or two. Or three. (Even Hiking Boot girl can change her laces to purple, non?)

to flip-flop or not to flip-flop Flip-flops have become the center of some controversy as they have morphed from strictly poolside to all-occasion wear. While some women feel it perfectly acceptable to don a pair of flips with their suit when going to work in the summer (ew!), some, like me, find that choice downright offensive. Wherever you stand on the issue, there are exponential options to choose from, including flip-flops with a low kitten heel of molded rubber for a more dressy occasion or terry-covered flip-flops for a spa day.

vintage I love to get my hands on a good vintage find. A vintage shoe is a worldly accessory, one that walked miles and lived another life before finding its way to you. The drawback, of course, is that aged heel - a bit dry with a tendency to crack or split, sometimes at very inopportune times. (Note to self: Do not wear vintage stilettos when accepting your Oscar.)

wedgies Wedge heels are a wonderful invention. They give you height and often are more cushy and comfortable than a sharp stiletto heel. They also add a bit of 1940s vintage glamour to any look. Just be careful of tipping to the side when walking - very high wedges can cause a fracture!

meow! The kitten heel, an exceedingly popular alternative to the high heel, denotes both a shape and a height. "Kitten" can mean anywhere from a quarter inch to a two-and-a-quarter-inch heel and is reminiscent of an hourglass in shape. Meow! Kitten heels, which always add an extra touch of femininity, are found on boots, ballet flat-style shoes, pointy toe skimmers, and, where they originally started, mules. A kitten is an acceptable alternative to a stiletto any day.

touch me, feel me Texture = Mmmmmmm. love to feel smooth satins or the heaviness of a metallic link, and see the twinkle of a rhinestone-studded heel. Texture plays a big role in expressing your inner sole. If you are hankering for a certain pair of shoes, see if they are available in a more interesting texture. Both your foot and your Sole Mate will thank you.

ACKNOWLEDGMENTS

Thanks to everyone who always shows their unfailing support on the journey of shoe. Your belief, love, support and humor are the absolute best I could ask for.

Mom, Dad, Patrick and Stacie, and my entire loving family of cheerleaders and supporters - every Pressel, Cline, King, Cleary aunt, uncle, cousin, godmothers and fathers! My godson Dan, Grandma Cline, and Kit King and her YSL platforms with lucite heels. I love you.

Lora, JJ and Willem Appleton; Jason Campbell; Tim Clark; Bill Cline; Genevieve Cline; Mary Donnelly; Heidi Ewing; Kristin and John Hall; Amy Holman; Patricia Handschiegel; Ruthie Wells Kaminskas; Jessica Zacholl, Carmen Hernandez: Holly and EmmyLou Waterfield; Sarah Lukashok; Raymond McDaniel; Wendy and Sunny Shanker; Ann Marie Simonelli; Jason & Randy Sklar; Jessica Zucker, Griffin: I love you all so much!

Very special thanks to Mary Gnetz and the team at Lightning Source, to Peter Ratcliffe who made my words sing in a brilliant layout, colors and design, and Mary Pressel Cline who made every shoe girl come alive with true personality and panache.

In very loving memory of Helen Pressel, Jim and Jane Cleary, and Bob King, who all taught me such important life lessons.